Scripture of the Week

Proverbs 3:6 – "In all thy ways acknowledge Him, and He shall direct thy paths." (KJV)

Mrs. Christian's Daycare

DIRECT THY PATH

Published by Teaching Parables

Copyright ©2022 Tiffiney Rogers-McDaniel

www.teachingparables.com

www.tiffineyrogers-mcdaniel.com

ISBN #978-1-7354173-5-6

This book is sold subject to the condition that it shall not, by way of trade or otherwise, be lent, scanned, photocopied, resold, hired out or otherwise circulated without the publisher's prior consent in any form of binding or cover other than that in which it is published and without a similar condition including this condition being imposed on the subsequent publisher.

The moral right of the author has been asserted.

Illustrations Copyright © Tiffiney Rogers-McDaniel

Illustrations by Mariya Rana

As the kids finish up lunch, Mrs. Christian decides they will do something different today. She wants to do a little demonstration of the scripture for the week to make sure the kids have a good understanding of what the verse means.

"Okay, boys and girls, let's settle down and take a seat on the floor. Today we are going to play a little game that will help you see and understand the scripture that you have worked so hard to learn this week, but first, who can recite this week's scripture?"

"I can," Hope says, waving her hand in excitement.

Mrs. Christian says, "Great! Come to the front of the class and recite the scripture for us."

As Hope moves to the front of the class, she notices that Mrs. Christian is gathering up many different objects.

Hope begins, "Proverbs chapter three verse six says, 'In all thy ways acknowledge Him, and He shall direct thy paths.'"

Mrs. Christian praises Hope for the outstanding job she did and asks Hope if she would like to help demonstrate the scripture to the class.

Hope's friends Faith and Charity are her biggest cheerleaders, so they clap and cheer when Hope says yes.

"This is what we're going to do," says Mrs. Christian. "I am going to place this blindfold across your eyes and tie it in the back. I need you to listen closely to my voice and only do what I tell you to do.

If you hear any other voice, you should ignore it completely. Does that make sense?"

"Yes, I understand," says Hope.

"Are you ready, then?" Mrs. Christian asks.

"Yes, I'm ready," Hope answers.

Mrs. Christian leads Hope to the chair in the middle of the floor and has her sit down.

"Okay, Hope, for your first direction, I want you to stand up."

Hope giggles and stands up.

Mrs. Christian says, "Now I want you to take five steps forward."

Hope walks forward as the class counts out loud. "One, two, three, four, five."

Mrs. Christian continues, "Bend down and pick up an object off the floor."

Hope bends down and feels around, finding and picking up the object from the floor. It is a book, and she holds it in her right hand.

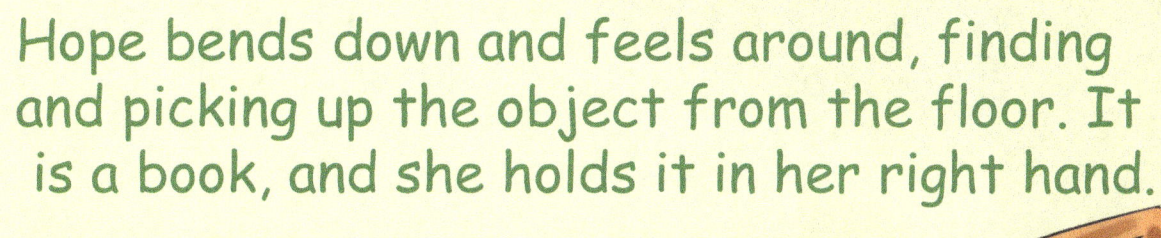

Ms. Lovejoy, Mrs. Christian's assistant, says, "Take two steps backward, Hope."

Hope hesitates because she knows that isn't Mrs. Christian's voice. She shakes her head and puts her hand on her hip. "Oh, no, that's not Mrs. Christian. That's Ms. Lovejoy's voice. You can't fool me!"

The class erupts in laughter, and Mrs. Christian says, "Good job, Hope! You're almost there. Now, turn to the right."

Hope turns to the right.

Then Ms. Lovejoy says, "Turn to the left."

Hope starts to turn back but then stops and says, "No, you can't fool me, Ms. Lovejoy!"

Good job," says Mrs. Christian. "I want you to take your right foot, raise it up, stretch it out, and place it on the floor."

Hope does exactly as instructed, holding the position with her feet spread out.

"I want you to lift your left foot and bring it up beside your right foot," Mrs. Christian says.

Hope is now standing straight again.

"Take two more steps forward."

The class counts again. "One, two."

"Put your book in your left hand." Mrs. Christian waits until Hope obeys, then she says, "Now stretch your right hand out like you're about to grab something."

The class cheers for Hope. Mrs. Christian takes the blindfold off, and Hope smiles. She's standing right in front of the treasure chest, her hand poised to collect her reward.

"I am so proud of you, Hope. You did a great job! And for being such a good sport, go ahead and grab two rewards from the treasure chest—one for reciting the scripture, and one for following my directions so well."

After Hope chooses her two items from the chest and joins the other kids on the floor, Mrs. Christian explains how important it is to know God's voice. "Hope was blindfolded and couldn't see where she was going, but she made it through by listening and obeying my instructions. Remember how she started sitting down?"

The kids all nod their heads.

"It was impossible for her to move forward. She had to stand up and take steps to get where she was going. Who can tell me what would have happened if Hope had listened to Ms. Lovejoy?"

Several kids raise their hands, and Mrs. Christian points to Faith. "She would have run into something and gotten hurt!"

"That's right!" Mrs. Christian agrees. "This shows how important it is to listen to the right person. Did you see what she picked up on her journey? Hope, show us what's in your lap."

Hope stands up and holds out her Bible so the class can see.

"Class, every direction you need is in there. The Bible is our roadmap for life. Hope made the right turns and even stepped over obstacles that could've tripped her up because she followed good instructions from a familiar voice. By listening to my voice, Hope made it to the treasure chest, which is full of different blessings. So, boys and girls, take the time to listen to God's voice and follow his directions, and he will lead you the right way every time."

The End

Teaching Parables is a collection of personalized children's books that gives real life examples of bible verses to help the readers learn and build a foundation of good values, strong faith, and to share God's Word for generations to come!

This set of faith-based books aims to reach adults and children to remind and show them God's promises and goodness. These bible stories will teach children how to apply biblical lessons to their daily lives and help to assist them in establishing success spiritually, mentally and physically.

Please feel free to check out the other books in our collection @ www.teachingparables.com.

Send us your pictures!
Have a cute picture of your child reading one of our books? We would love to see them. Submit them to tiffiney@teachingparables.com for a chance to be featured on the website and/or social media pages!

Facebook@teachingparables
Instagram@tiffineymcdaniel

We love reviews!
If you loved this book or any of the books in our collection, please feel free to go to Amazon and write a review. If you loved it, I'm sure someone else will too! Let's spread the Word!

www.ingramcontent.com/pod-product-compliance
Lightning Source LLC
Chambersburg PA
CBHW081159070526
44583CB00021B/2909